Our World

Solar Power

By Sarah Levete

Aladdin/Watts
London • Sydney

Designed and produced by
Aladdin Books Ltd
2/3 Fitzroy Mews
London W1T 6DF

First published in 2006 by
Franklin Watts
338 Euston Road
London NW1 3BH

Franklin Watts Australia
Hachette Children's Books
Level 17/207 Kent Street
Sydney NSW 2000

A catalogue record for this
book is available from the
British Library.

ISBN 0 7496 6280 8

Printed in Malaysia

Editor:
Harriet Brown

Designer:
Flick, Book Design and Graphics
Simon Morse

Consultants:
Jackie Holderness – former Senior Lecturer
in Primary Education, Westminster Institute,
Oxford Brookes University

Rob Bowden – education consultant, author
and photographer specialising in social and
environmental issues.

Illustrations:
Ian Thompson

Picture researcher:
Alexa Brown

Photocredits:
Abbreviations: l-left, r-right, b-bottom, t-top, c-centre,
m-middle. Back cover – www.istockphoto.com /
Nicholas Belton. Front cover – Corel. 19tr – Alan
Jackson, Aidworld, Cambridge and Ben Newland,
University of Brighton, 18bl – BP Angola, 6tr –
Comstock, 7ml, 28bl, 30tr – Corbis, 18tr, 25br –
Corel, 28tl – EnviroMission, 29tl – Falmouth Scientific
and AUSI, 14tr – Gaiasolar Hungary kft. Photo by T.
Veghely, 20tl, 21br, 29br – NASA, 3bl, 20tl – Photo
by Solar Sailor, 4ml, 24tl – Photodisc, 6bl, 7bl, 10tr –
Select Pictures, 22tr – www.solarcentury.com, 15bl –
Solar-factory CORP, Freiburg, 3mtl, 5tl, 15tr –
Stockbyte, 1, 3tl, 4bl, 5bl, 5tr, 10bl, 11tr, 13tl, 20tl,
23bl, 24bl, 25tl, 26bl, 30br, 31tl – US Department of
Energy, 17tl – Voltaic Systems, 14bl, 22bl, 23tr, 27tr –
www.iea-pvps.org, 12bl – www.istockphoto.com /
Blaine Walulik, 9tl – www.istockphoto.com / Christine
Gonsalves, 2-3 – www.istockphoto.com / Eli
Mordechai, 8bl – www.istockphoto.com / Nicholas
Belton, 5br, 16bl, 31bl – www.istockphoto.com /
Pamela Hodson, 7tr – www.istockphoto.com / Pauline
Wilson, 8tl – www.istockphoto.com / Shae Cardenas,
26tr – www.istockphoto.com / Shaun Lowe, 3mbl, 12tl
– www.istockphoto.com / Thomas Pullicino, 5ml, 16tl,
30mr – www.scsolar.com

CONTENTS

Notes to parents and teachers

This series has been developed for group use in the classroom as well as for children reading on their own. In particular, its differentiated text allows children of mixed abilities to enjoy reading about the same topic. The larger size text (A, below) offers apprentice readers a simplified text. This simplified text is used in the introduction to each chapter and in the picture captions. This font is part of the © Sassoon family of fonts recommended by the National Literacy Early Years Strategy document for maximum legibility. The smaller size text (B, below) offers a more challenging read for older or more able readers.

Benefits of solar energy

The Sun shines across our world every day. It will continue to do so for many millions of years.

A

 This solar power plant uses free energy from the Sun.

The Sun belongs to everyone, all over the world, so we can all use its energy.

B

Questions, key words and glossary

Each spread ends with a question which parents and teachers can use to discuss and develop further ideas and concepts. Further questions are provided in a quiz on page 30. A reduced version of pages 30 and 31 is shown below. The illustrated 'Key words' section is provided as a revision tool, particularly for apprentice readers, in order to help with spelling, writing and guided reading as part of the literacy hour. The glossary is for more able or older readers. In addition to the glossary's role as a reference aid, it is also designed to reinforce new vocabulary and provide a tool for further discussion and revision. When glossary terms first appear in the text they are highlighted in bold.

 See how much you know!

What is the Sun?

What does PV stand for?

Which colour soaks up the most heat?

How does solar energy work at night-time?

How can we use the Sun's heat to produce electricity?

What needs to happen to encourage more people to turn to solar power?

Why is solar energy a 'green' energy source?

Which vehicles can run on solar power?

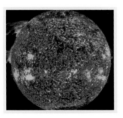

Key words
Panel

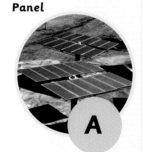

Mirror   **Power**

Solar   **Sunlight**

Battery

Glossary

Concentrate – To collect in one place to make very hot.
Electrons – Tiny particles that flow to produce electricity.
Generate – To make or produce.
Heat exchanger – Where heated liquid sends its heat to water.
Photovoltaic – To do with light (photo) and electricity (volt).
Portable – Something that can be easily carried.
Power plant – A place where lots of electricity is produced from the Sun's energy.
Recharge – To replace energy that has been used.
Solar array – A group of solar panels.
Solar cell – An object that is used to change sunlight into electricity.

What is solar energy?

The Sun covers our planet in light and warmth. A mixture of heat and light from the Sun can be used as energy to heat water and make machines work. Energy from the Sun is called solar energy. Solar means to do with the Sun.

◀ **Energy makes things work. You need energy to throw a ball.**

Without energy, nothing works. Everything needs energy. There are many types of energy. The Sun's energy helps plants and flowers to grow. We eat plants and other foods. The energy from food gives us the energy to throw a ball and run around.

▶ The Sun's heat dries wet clothes.

The Sun is packed with energy. In one hour, the Earth receives more energy from the Sun than the whole world uses in a year. This energy can also be used to **generate** electricity. We call this electricity solar power.

The Sun is a blazing star.

This huge burning ball of gas is our nearest star. Even though it is 150 million km away from Earth, the Sun can shine so brightly that you need to shade your eyes from its light. Sunlight can feel hot on your skin. You need to wear suncream to protect your skin.

What would happen if the Sun stopped shining?

Heat from the Sun

What happens to the water in a paddling pool on a sunny day? The Sun makes it warm enough to lie in without shivering. This energy from the Sun can heat the water for hot baths and showers. Heat from the Sun can be used to heat houses too.

◀ **Sunlight shines through glass in this greenhouse.**

Fruits such as tomatoes and exotic plants grow well in a hot greenhouse. The Sun's light and heat pass through the clear glass windows. When the light and heat are trapped inside the greenhouse, it feels very warm.

◀ The Sun can be used to heat up water.

Buildings can be fitted with pipes and plates that collect the Sun's heat on the roof. These contain a liquid that heats up quickly when the Sun shines on it. The hot liquid is used to heat water. The hot water is sent through pipes to taps, ready for use.

Some colours soak up the Sun's heat better than others.

Paint some paper plates different colours, including one black and one white. Put them out in the sunshine for a few hours, and then check which one is hottest, and which one is coolest. Black clothes absorb the Sun's heat and make you feel even hotter. Solar pipes and plates are black so that they soak up lots of heat.

 Which colour is best to wear on a hot day?

Electricity from the Sun's energy

The Sun's energy can be used to make heat and electricity. Special mirrors gather the Sun's energy. This energy creates heat. The heat is used to turn water into steam. Steam is used to produce electricity.

◀ **Mirrors collect sunlight.**

Mirrors **concentrate** sunlight in one place. In a solar power tower, lots of mirrors reflect sunlight onto a special collector. The collector is filled with a liquid. The liquid stays hot for a long time. It is pumped into containers. When power is needed, the liquid flows to a **heat exchanger** where it heats water and produces steam. The steam turns a turbine that makes electrical energy.

These curved mirrors turn to follow the Sun.

Power troughs have mirrored surfaces. They turn to follow the Sun. Sunlight heats a liquid-filled pipe in the centre of the troughs. This is sent to a heat exchanger. The steam produced is used to create electricity.

Steam from hot water turns a turbine.

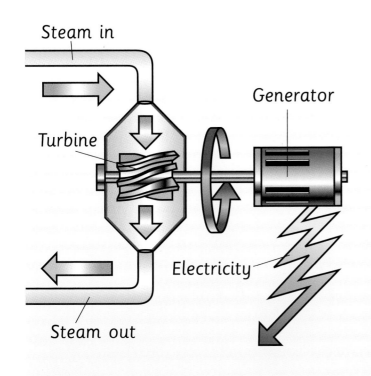

Steam in

Generator

Turbine

Electricity

Steam out

Sunlight is used to boil a liquid that heats up quickly. Steam from the boiling liquid powers a turbine. A turbine is like a water-wheel which is powered by steam instead of water. The turbine drives a generator which produces electricity for homes, offices and factories.

 How have you used electricity today?

Electricity from sunlight

There are other ways that the Sun's energy is used to make electricity. Have a look at this calculator (left). At the top, above the numbers, there is a row of solar cells. They use energy directly from the Sun to make the calculator work.

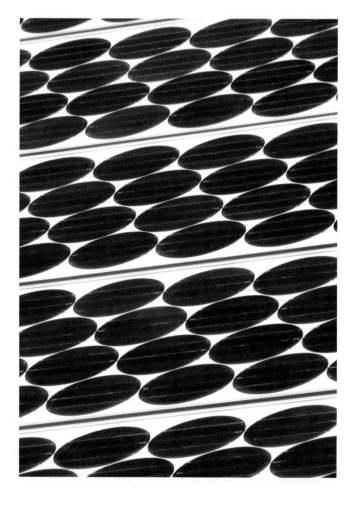

◀ **These solar cells turn sunlight into electricity.**

The proper name for **solar cells** is **photovoltaic** cells, or PV cells for short. Photo means to do with light and voltaic means to do with electricity. Just one PV cell can power a calculator or wristwatch.

◀ Solar panels are made up of solar cells.

A group of connected solar cells is called a **solar panel**. Between 10 and 20 solar panels grouped together are called a **solar array**. Solar panels or arrays work best when they face the sunlight.

Solar cells are made from a type of melted sand called silicon.

When sunlight shines on a solar cell, the Sun's energy makes tiny particles called **electrons** jump around. When the electrons jump from one layer of silicon to another in the solar cell, electricity is created. The electricity can power a lamp or machine.

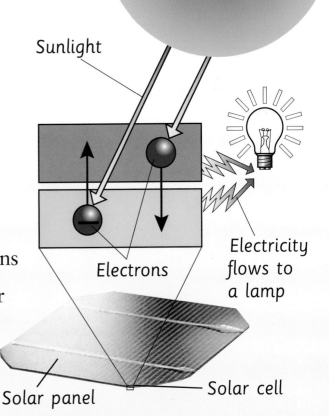

Sunlight

Electricity flows to a lamp

Electrons

Solar panel

Solar cell

Why do solar panels move to face the Sun?

Packed with power

Solar cells make enough energy to power this torch (right). Hundreds of solar cells connected together make enough electricity for homes and offices, or to keep small villages supplied with electricity.

◀ **Electricity from these solar cells keeps buildings heated and lit.**

This housing area in the city of Amersfoort in The Netherlands runs on electricity from solar cells. It is one of the largest solar-powered housing projects in the world. It also includes solar-powered schools and a sports centre.

▶ This space station uses solar power.

High above the Earth, solar power is used to keep spacecraft working. The solar panels create enough electricity to power the International Space Station, a large spacecraft where astronauts live and work.

Making a solar cell uses up a lot of energy.

Making solar cells is expensive and uses up energy. It takes up to four years to create enough energy from one solar cell to make up for the amount of energy used to create it! In the future, the cost of making solar cells may come down.

 Can you think of other objects powered by solar cells?

Storing the Sun's power

There are times when we need a lot of electricity, and there are times when we need very little electricity. To make sure we have electricity when we need it, scientists have discovered ways to store solar power.

◀ **These lamps store solar power.**

A battery is a store of energy. Solar cells can store energy from the Sun in a battery. The battery releases the electricity when it is needed, such as at night. During the day, the solar cells replace the energy that has been used from the battery. This is called **recharging**.

◄ **The Sun powers up batteries in this back-pack.**

Solar-powered back-packs can provide **portable** power for a music machine or a computer. During the day, sunlight recharges the batteries for the music machine or computer. Carrying a supply of energy in a back-pack is useful for people living or travelling in remote places.

Solar power works best in hot and sunny countries.

Places that receive lots of sunshine have the most useful solar power systems. But even in hot countries, the Sun does not shine at night. Solar power can be stored in batteries or it can be used alongside other fuels such as natural gas.

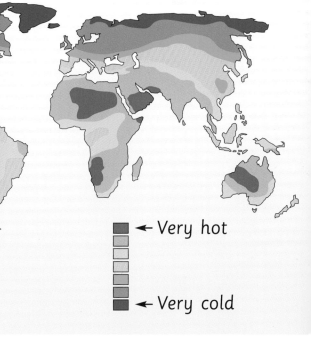

← Very hot

← Very cold

 How does a solar-powered radio work at night?

Solar power in remote places

Solar power is especially useful for people in some remote areas of the world. Here, there may be no power stations and no network of gas or oil pipes to provide fuel for electricity.

◀ **This village in Angola, Africa, runs on solar power.**

Solar energy is helping this village recover from the effects of war. Solar power provides street lighting and lighting for community buildings, such as the school and medical centre. It provides power for a freshwater pumping system and for hospital fridges that contain important medicines that need to be kept cool.

► Computers can be powered by solar cells.

You probably use computers at school and at home. But in some parts of the world, there is no electrical supply to power computers. Solar-powered computers make it possible for more people there to use computers.

The Sun's energy can cook a meal.

Mirrored surface

Rays of sunlight

Heat

Food

The Sun's rays can be focused to create intense heat for cooking. A mirror or solar box cooker traps the Sun's heat. The trapped heat cooks the food. Solar cookers mean that people do not have to collect and use up firewood for cooking.

? What would your life be like without electricity?

On the move

Today we travel across the world in cars, boats and aeroplanes. Most of these vehicles use fuels, such as diesel and petrol. Burning these fuels releases harmful chemicals into the air. Solar power can keep us on the move and it causes less pollution.

◀ Cars can fill up on sunshine.

Solar-powered cars don't use petrol – they use sunshine. Hundreds of solar cells turn sunlight into electricity to power the car's engine. There are even solar car races. In the American Solar Challenge, cars travel over 3,000 km across the USA, running on sunshine.

◀ Sunlight could push spacecraft through space.

In the future, the Sun may be used to power spacecraft through space. A spacecraft would still need rockets to help it leave Earth. Once in space, sunlight would physically push on the sails to propel the craft forwards.

The Sun powers this plane.

This solar-powered aircraft is piloted by remote control. It can stay in the air for a long time to study weather patterns. The wings are covered with solar panels, providing the electricity for the aircraft's motors. A battery provides power so the plane can fly during the night.

 Why is solar power better for the environment?

Our solar world

Roadside telephones, parking meters, flashing road signs and lights in bus shelters can all run on solar power. Houses, flats, offices and schools can all use solar energy to meet their energy needs.

◀ **Some schools are powered by the Sun.**

Schools spend about three times more on energy than on books! Using solar power means there could be more money for books. The Star School in Arizona, USA, is completely powered by solar energy. It provides all the school's power needs, keeps fridges cold and heats up lunches.

This building uses solar power.

Solar panels can have two uses. Firstly, they are used to generate electricity. Secondly, they can be used to shade the inside of the building. This stops the building from becoming too hot in the summer.

Energy from the Sun can be used to light a building.

Sunlight can be used to light and warm a building during the daytime (left). This type of energy is called passive solar energy. It reduces the use of electricity, which may come from burning fuels. Some buildings are specially designed to trap solar energy in this way.

How would you design a building to trap solar power?

Benefits of solar energy

The Sun shines across our world every day. It will continue to do so for many millions of years. Mirrors, solar cells and specially designed buildings make it possible for us to use the Sun to supply some of our energy needs.

◀ **This solar power plant uses free energy from the Sun.**

The Sun belongs to everyone, all over the world, so we can all use its energy. Although sunlight is free, solar cells are expensive to make and it is costly to set up a solar power system such as a **solar power plant**. However, when it is built, there is very little to go wrong with a solar power system – it just needs the Sun!

◀ Solar power is a 'green' energy source.

It does not cause pollution by burning fuel and it does not make lots of noise. However, it is not perfect. To make a solar cell, rocks must be dug out of the ground and made ready to use. This uses up energy.

The Sun will last for millions of years. Other fuels will run out.

The most commonly used sources of fuel are coal, gas and oil. When we burn these fuels, they cause pollution. These fuels are also running out. When we have used them up, it will take millions of years for more coal, gas and oil to form under the ground. The Sun will continue to shine and provide power.

 How would hospitals and schools benefit from solar power?

Alternative energy

Many people prefer to use energy sources that do not harm the natural world. These are often called alternative energy sources. Solar energy, wind energy and water energy are alternative energy sources.

◀ **These turbines use wind energy to create electricity.**

Heat from the Sun warms the air around our planet. The warm air rises. As it does so, cool air sinks. The movement of air forms wind, which turns wind turbines. These turbines turn a generator, and this creates electricity. A group of wind turbines is called a wind farm.

▶ Solar power can be used with other energy sources.

Sometimes, solar power systems have a 'back-up' energy supply for times when energy from the Sun is not enough. This may be other alternative energies, such as wind or water energy, or it may be a fossil fuel such as natural gas.

This machine is called a tokamak. It makes energy by copying the Sun.

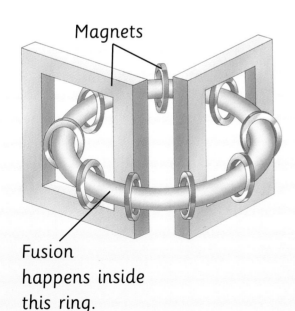

Magnets

Fusion happens inside this ring.

The Sun makes its energy by joining, or fusing, atoms together in a process called fusion. For this to happen, the atoms have to be heated to 100 million °C. A machine called a tokamak has carried out fusion trials. A much larger version is being built in France by international teams and could provide a source of alternative energy.

 Why do you think some people do not like wind farms?

The future of solar energy

Scientists are looking for other ways to use solar energy safely and effectively. Could this experimental solar greenhouse tower produce enough warm air to rise up, drive a turbine and produce electricity?

◀ In the future, solar cells may be sprayed onto road surfaces.

At the moment, solar cells are fitted onto hard panels. Advances in science may lead to solar cells that can be sprayed onto cars or road surfaces. Soft material could also be fitted with solar cells to cover any shape of house or building.

◀ **This solar-powered boat can study the oceans.**

This boat floats on the surface during the day to recharge its solar cells. At night it can use the stored power to dive down deep to study the oceans. Lots of the Sun's energy is trapped in the oceans. Scientists hope that one day a sea solar power plant could be used to create electricity.

The Sun shines on the Moon.

Scientists want to put solar collectors on the Moon and other planets to trap the Sun's energy. The energy could be used to create electricity for humans on any planet.

 How *else* could we use the Sun's energy in the future?

See how much you know!

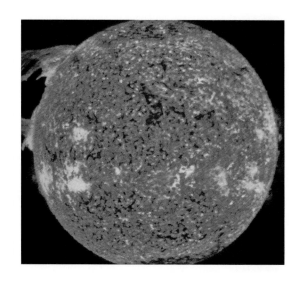

What is the Sun?

What does PV stand for?

Which colour soaks up the most heat?

How does solar energy work at night-time?

How can we use the Sun's heat to produce electricity?

What needs to happen to encourage more people to turn to solar power?

Why is solar energy a 'green' energy source?

Which vehicles can run on solar power?

Key words

Panel

Electricity   **Generator**

Power   **Solar**

Sunshine   **Turbine**

Battery

Glossary

Concentrate – To collect in one place to make very hot.

Electrons – Tiny particles that flow to produce electricity.

Generate – To make or produce.

Heat exchanger – Where heated liquid sends its heat to water.

Photovoltaic – To do with light (photo) and electricity (volt).

Portable – Something that can be easily carried.

Recharge – To replace energy that has been used.

Solar array – A group of solar panels.

Solar cell – An object that is used to change sunlight into electricity.

Solar panel – A group of connected solar cells.

Solar power plant – A place where lots of electricity is produced from the Sun's energy.

Index